Brief

Encounters

Women's Underwear and the Classic Age of

PRION

IN ASSOCIATION WITH THE ADVERTISING ARCHIVES

First published in 2001
Reprinted 2004 by

Prion
an imprint of the
Carlton Publishing Group
20 Mortimer Street
London W1T 3JW

Compilation © Prion Books 2001

ISBN 1-85375-443-9

All images courtesy of The Advertising Archives, London
Many thanks to Suzanne and Emma

Printed and bound in China
By Leo Paper Products Ltd

Warner's Rust-Proof Corsets

The artist has been able to portray this beautiful figure because of the perfect corseting of the model.

The designing and boning are the vital parts of the corset. These you cannot see. For their value you must depend upon our word and the word of your merchant, and your knowledge must come through actual wear.

All we ask is that you try Warner's Corsets. Give them hard wear. You will find all parts equal to whatever wearing strain may be put upon them.

The Warner policy is to make corsets so perfect in pattern, workmanship and material that no part will become useless until the whole garment is worn out.

There is a *shaping power* in a Warner's Model which must be appreciated by every woman, whatever her figure. The attached hose supporters, now an integral part of the corset, are the

Security
Rubber Button
Hose Supporters

Sold everywhere

$1 to $7 per pair
Every Pair Guaranteed
The Warner Brothers Company
New York   Chicago   San Francisco

EVERY PAIR GUARANTEED.

Prion Books Ltd. Imperial Works, Perren Street, London NW5 3ED
for information email humour@prion.co.uk • image courtesy of the advertising archives

Prion Books Ltd. Imperial Works, Perren Street, London NW5 3ED
for information email humour@prion.co.uk • image courtesy of the advertising archives

Ad Nauseam

Dress created especially for Sarong by Polly Hornburg. "Calypso", Bermuda. Shown, style 108, high-waisted Sarong, sizes 24 to 34, $10.95. Other styles to size 44, from $4.95.

she's wearing a **sarong**®

the criss-cross girdle that walks and never rides up

In all the world, there is no girdle like Sarong. Only Sarong shapes you slenderly, caters comfortably to your every movement. Only Sarong's patented, hidden construction lifts and flattens your tummy youthfully. Only Sarong's exclusive criss-cross feature lets you walk, stand, sit or bend with complete freedom all day—every day. You'll forget that you're wearing a girdle till admiring eyes remind you! **Free!** Sarong's new booklet "Facts about Figures." Write Sarong, Inc., Department L-2, Box 306, New Haven 2, Connecticut.

sarong
the patented girdle
with the criss-cross front

"SARONG is the registered trademark of Sarong, Inc. for its girdles."

Prion Books Ltd. Imperial Works, Perren Street, London NW5 3ED
for information email humour@prion.co.uk • image courtesy of the advertising archives

Prion Books Ltd. Imperial Works, Perren Street, London NW5 3ED
for information email humour@prion.co.uk • image courtesy of the advertising archives

Figure Reduction without dieting!

Grow slender—feel comfortable—look younger! It's so easy if you wear the new W.B. Rubber Reduso.

No more starvation diet—no need for violent exercise. Easily, naturally, imperceptibly, the W.B. Rubber Reduso massages away the superfluous flesh.

Made in pure Para Rubber. Healthy, hygienic, washable again and again.

From all good drapers, or write for illustrated folder to :

W. B. CORSETS (Dept. 420), **23 London Wall, London, E.C.2**

Prion Books Ltd. Imperial Works, Perren Street, London NW5 3ED
for information email humour@prion.co.uk • image courtesy of the advertising archives

Prion Books Ltd. Imperial Works, Perren Street, London NW5 3ED
for information email humour@prion.co.uk • image courtesy of the advertising archives

Ad
Nauseam

Prion Books Ltd. Imperial Works, Perren Street, London NW5 3ED
for information email humour@prion.co.uk • image courtesy of the advertising archives

Ad Nauseam

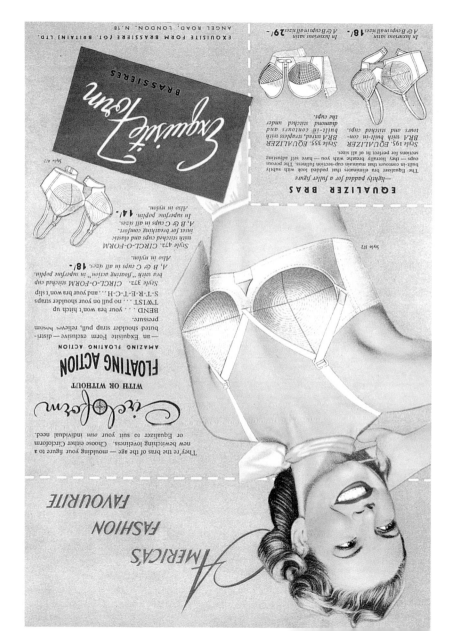

AMERICA'S FASHION FAVOURITE

They're the bras of the age — moulding your figure to a new bewitching loveliness. Choose either Circloform or Equalizer to suit your *own* individual need.

Circloform

WITH OR WITHOUT
FLOATING ACTION

AMAZING FLOATING ACTION

FLOATING ACTION —an Exquisite Form exclusive — distributed shoulder strap pull, relieves bosom pressure.

BEND ... your bra won't hitch up
TWIST ... no pull on your shoulder straps
S-T-R-E-T-C-H ... and your bra won't slip

Style 371. CIRCL-O-FORM stitched cup bra with "floating action" in superfine poplin. A, B & C cups in all sizes. **18/-**. Also in nylon.

Style 472. CIRCL-O-FORM with stitched cups and elastic inset for breathing comfort. A, B & C cups in all sizes. In superfine poplin. **14/-**. Also in nylon.

Style 371

Style 472

EQUALIZER BRAS
—*lightly padded for a fuller figure*

The Equalizer bra eliminates that padded look with subtly built-in contours that maintain cup-section fullness. The porous cups — they literally breathe with you — have self adjusting sections for perfect fit in of all sizes.

Style 195. EQUALIZER BRA with built-in contours and diamond stitched under the cups.

Style 355. EQUALIZER BRA wired, strapless with built-in contours and diamond stitched cups.

In luxurious satin **18/-** *A & B cup small sizes*

In luxurious satin **29/-** *A & B cup small sizes*

Exquisite Form
BRASSIERES

EXQUISITE FORM BRASSIERE (GT. BRITAIN) LTD.
ANGEL ROAD, LONDON, N.18

Prion Books Ltd. Imperial Works, Perren Street, London NW5 3ED
for information email humour@prion.co.uk • image courtesy of the advertising archives

Ad Nauseam

Un-Mentionables?

.. *Not* this kind

of MUNSING *Wear*

*We're very proud to tell you about
these smart new underfashions*

THERE'S such a lot to say about the new things that Munsingwear
makes! And about their slim smartness and trim tailoring. The
garments above . . . a daring "bare-back" one-piece chemise, and the
Munsingwear "Sketchies" . . . a new bandeau and pantie set . . . are
but two of the many new Munsingwear Underfashions of specially
processed Munsingwear Rayon. We only wish we could show you
all! You'll like their quality and their prices. Typically Munsingwear.
See them in a good store near you. Munsingwear, Minneapolis.

*Munsingwear makes all styles of smart undergarments in all types of fabrics. For
men, women and children.* UNDERWEAR · WATERWEAR · HOSIERY · SLEEPING
AND LOUNGING GARMENTS · KNIT COATS · PULL-ONS · FOUNDATION GARMENTS

LET   MUNSINGWEAR   COVER   YOU   WITH   SATISFACTION

Prion Books Ltd. Imperial Works, Perren Street, London NW5 3ED
for information email humour@prion.co.uk • image courtesy of the advertising archives

AT LAST -

Prion Books Ltd. Imperial Works, Perren Street, London NW5 3ED
for information email humour@prion.co.uk • image courtesy of the advertising archives

Prion Books Ltd. Imperial Works, Perren Street, London NW5 3ED
for information email humour@prion.co.uk • image courtesy of the advertising archives

Ad Nauseam

THE CORSET
THAT GLOWS
IN THE DARK

Paris Photos by SAVITRY

THE CORSET BY DAY

It is made of white elastic lace and nylon (specially treated). It is appliquéd with two high-climbing pale green tulips, outlined in washable gold paint.

Cried Dior when he introduced the shorter skirt and straight 'princess' line: "I am sick of seeing women cased up in iron. . . . I have done away with the corset!"

Corset manufacturers knew better! Monsieur Dior's mannequins might possess flat diaphragms and minuscule hips; most of their clients did not. As a compromise, there is less whaleboning.

New York produces a revolutionary new 'sarong'-like girdle (see over), which has no bones. Paris goes two better, and presents the boneless girdle-cum-petticoat, and the Corset that glows in the dark

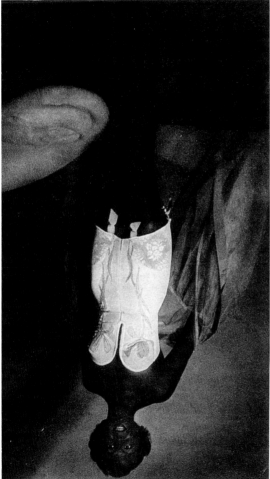

THE SAME PHOSPHORESCENT CORSET BY NIGHT

By night, it is called 'Nuit de Feu' (Night of Fire), and it lives up to its name. Though this photograph was taken with infra-red light (to bring out the detail) the corset actually glows in the dark as long as it is 'charged' (exposed to the light) each day. It will be available in the more exclusive London shops in the spring . . . if the buyers think it will sell. Price: about 30 guineas.
Designer: 'Charmis Corsets, Paris.

Prion Books Ltd. Imperial Works, Perren Street, London NW5 3ED
for information email humour@prion.co.uk • image courtesy of the advertising archives

Ad Nauseam

caprice

PARIS | LONDON

"COCKTAIL" BRA (214) 36/-. PANTIE (956) 64/-. GIRDLE (863) 66/6.
Write for booklet — "Romance in Corsetry".
CAPRICE LIMITED, 3, NEW BURLINGTON STREET, LONDON, W.1.

"Romance in corsetry"

BRIEF ENCOUNTERS – WOMEN'S UNDERWEAR IN THE CLASSIC AGE OF ADVERTISING

Prion Books Ltd. Imperial Works, Perren Street, London NW5 3ED
for information email humour@prion.co.uk • image courtesy of the advertising archives

Ad Nauseam

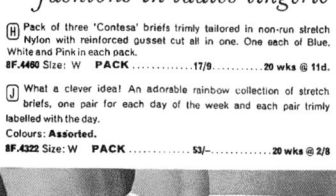

A brief statement of todays fashions in ladies lingerie

H Pack of three 'Contesa' briefs trimly tailored in non-run stretch Nylon with reinforced gusset cut all in one. One each of Blue, White and Pink in each pack.
8F.4460 Size: W   **PACK** ....17/9...........20 wks @ 11d.

J What a clever idea! An adorable rainbow collection of stretch briefs, one pair for each day of the week and each pair trimly labelled with the day.
Colours: **Assorted.**
8F.4322 Size: W   **PACK** .... 53/–............20 wks @ 2/8

G Stretch Leopard briefs, fashion fun for catlike confidence. Trim and snug fitting in patterned s-t-r-e-t-c-h Nylon.
Colour: **Leopard.**
8F.4461 Size: W   **BRIEFS**...........10/11...........20 wks @ 7d.

K Nudiult Brief Trio—a box of three pin-point eyelet briefs, one each in Primrose, Pink and Blue. Elasticated legs and double gusset give comfort with extra wear.
8F.4294 Size: W   **PACK** ....21/–............20 wks @ 1/–
8F.4295 Size: OS **PACK** ....24/–............20 wks @ 1/2

L Neat Threesome, in everyone's favourite colours, every pack contains three pairs of waffle briefs, one each in Sky, Pink and White. Styled with cuffed legs, in waffle interlock, the hardwearing undie fabric with an attractive raised design.
8F.4292 Size: W   **PACK** ....20/–............20 wks @ 1/–
8F.4293 Size: OS **PACK** ....22/7............20 wks @ 1/2

M Box of three Nylon briefs in assorted shades. Pink, Primrose and Blue. Ribbon threaded Lace highlights the front panel. Styled for comfort and wear, with a double gusset.
Colours: **Assorted.**
8F.5065 Size: W   **PACK**............. 21/–............20 wks @ 1/1

N 40 denier Nylon brief with insets of matching lace topping the elasticated leg. The double gusset is lined with interlock for comfort and wear.
Colours: **Lilac, Primrose, Pink, Black, Blue, White.**
8F.5063 Size: W   **BRIEF**............. 8/9............. 20 wks @ 6d.
8F.5064 Size: WX **BRIEF** ....9/9............. 20 wks @ 6d.

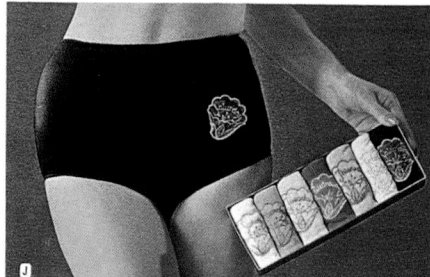

Contesa
PACK OF THREE

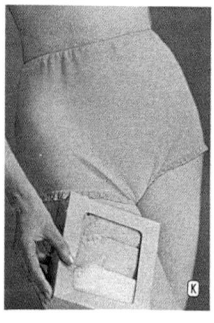

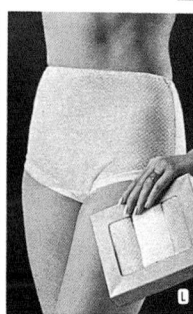

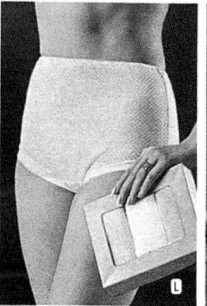

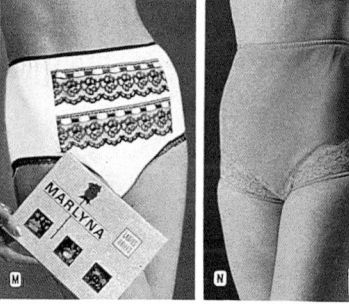

241

Prion Books Ltd. Imperial Works, Perren Street, London NW5 3ED
for information email humour@prion.co.uk • image courtesy of the advertising archives

Almost too good to throw away.

Zero disposable rayon panties.

ZERO
Throwaway panty
by Coupon
Regent Street London. Made in England

New Zero panties are everything you expect panties to be. They're soft. Delicate. Feminine.

They hug you snugly. And feel smooth to the touch. With all the strength you need. Zeros come in Pink. In White. In Blue.

They're everything you expect panties to be.

Everything.

But there's one thing that makes new Zeros different from any panty you've ever worn.

They're disposable.

So they're perfect for holidays. Ideal for all those times when you're caught out. You'll find a different advantage for Zero disposable rayon panties every day of the week.

Prion Books Ltd. Imperial Works, Perren Street, London NW5 3ED
for information email humour@prion.co.uk • image courtesy of the advertising archives

"Grippernickers"

The Panty Girdle
that comfortably holds up
long length stockings
without
suspenders

"Grippernickers" with stockings
wear like tights, except that if a run
starts you lose only one stocking.

"Grippernickers" means keeping your
stockings up and your tummy in.

"Grippernickers?" 25/-

by **Lovable** of course.

The Lovable Company Ltd., Faringdon Avenue, Harold Hill, Romford, Essex.

Prion Books Ltd. Imperial Works, Perren Street, London NW5 3ED
for information email humour@prion.co.uk • image courtesy of the advertising archives

Ad
Nauseam

Become a Lᴗvable
undercolour
agent (They're licensed to thrill)

Oh ! Oh ! 7 exciting colours have just entered your secret life ! Cool colours . . . hot colours . . . zingy colours. Here is Lovable's wonderful new colour co-ordinates concept. In Hot Pink, Cherry, Tangerine, Lemon, Apple, Turquoise, and Forget-me-not. Girdle 7300 and panty girdle 7301 in sizes Small, Medium and Large. Bra style 418 in sizes A32-36 and B32-38.

Left
Lightweight Lycra girdle match mated with all-nylon bra in luscious 'Hot Pink'.

Centre
Same whisper-weight Lycra in colourful Tangerine panty girdle. Matching nylon bra.

Right: This team of Lycra panty-girdle and nylon bra, in 'Apple Green'. Suspenders are detachable when you wear your panty-hose or stay up stockings.

Bras 13/11 Girdles 15/11 Panty Girdles 19/11

LOVABLE 'CAREFREE' COLOUR CO-ORDINATES

The Lovable Company Limited, Faringdon Avenue, Harold Hill, Romford, Essex

Prion Books Ltd. Imperial Works, Perren Street, London NW5 3ED
for information email humour@prion.co.uk • image courtesy of the advertising archives

Prion Books Ltd. Imperial Works, Perren Street, London NW5 3ED
for information email humour@prion.co.uk • image courtesy of the advertising archives

I dreamed I was

WANTED

in my Maidenform bra

Name: Star Flower*   **Reward:** Just wearing it!

Distinguishing characteristics: Circular stitched cups in pretty petal pattern. Twin elastic bands beneath cups. Upper bands adjust to make bra fit like custom-made. Lower bands make bra breathe with wearer.

Physical description: White broadcloth. A, B, C cups. 2.50.

Last seen: In stores everywhere. Looking *ravishing*.

Prion Books Ltd. Imperial Works, Perren Street, London NW5 3ED
for information email humour@prion.co.uk • image courtesy of the advertising archives

I dreamed
I went
to work
in my
maidenform bra

CHANSONETTE* with famous 'circular-spoke' stitching

Notice <u>two</u> patterns of stitching on the cups of this bra? Circles that uplift and support, spokes that discreetly emphasize your curves. This fine detailing shapes your figure naturally—keeps the bra shapely, even after machine-washing. The triangular cut-out between the cups gives you extra "breathing room" as the lower elastic insert expands. In white or black: A, B, C cups. **2.00**

Other styles: Broadcloth: Cotton, "Dacron" Polyester 2.50; Lace, 3.50; with all-elastic back, 3.00; Contour, 3.00; Full-length, 3.50.

*REG. U.S. PAT. OFF. ©1964 BY **Maidenform, Inc.**, makers of bras, girdles, swimwear, and active sportswear.

Prion Books Ltd. Imperial Works, Perren Street, London NW5 3ED
for information email humour@prion.co.uk • image courtesy of the advertising archives

Ad Nauseam

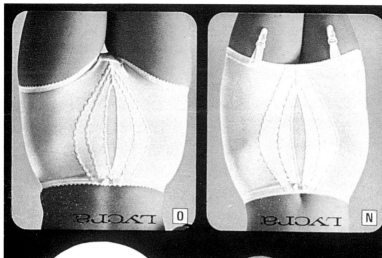

Prion Books Ltd. Imperial Works, Perren Street, London NW5 3ED
for information email humour@prion.co.uk • image courtesy of the advertising archives

Undies to be searched in.

Don't scoff.
In five minutes time you could get mistaken for a Secret Service courier. Handsome Colonel Fernandez, the infamous Transylvanian double agent, would search you thoroughly for the microfilm.

Blushmaking? Not if you're in Triumph undies. Get in some quick.

Triumph: bras, briefs, pantie-girdles, bra-slips, waist-slips, mini-slips and nighties — all in co-ordinating prints, plains and laces. Prices from only 8/11. Sizes 32 to 38.

Triumph.
Undies to be seen in.

Triumph INTERNATIONAL

Prion Books Ltd. Imperial Works, Perren Street, London NW5 3ED
for information email humour@prion.co.uk • image courtesy of the advertising archives

Prion Books Ltd. Imperial Works, Perren Street, London NW5 3ED
for information email humour@prion.co.uk • image courtesy of the advertising archives

Ad Nauseam

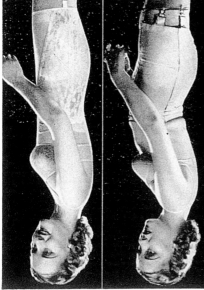

Prion Books Ltd. Imperial Works, Perren Street, London NW5 3ED
for information email humour@prion.co.uk • image courtesy of the advertising archives

THE BRA FOR YOU

'U' by *Silhouette*

GIVES YOU THE LOOK THAT HE ADMIRES

A bra should hold you, mould you; but it should do more. It should make you look more feminine, more vivacious, more alluring, so that you are looked at, envied, admired. All this, the 'U' bra by Silhouette will do for you—whatever your size or shape. Try one on today and see for yourself the difference it makes.

'U' STYLE 1 (SHAPED-BY-YOU) A cup 32", 34", 36". B and C cups 32", 34", 36", 38".

'U' STYLE 2 (PRE-SHAPED) A and B cups 32", 34", 36".

'U' STYLE 3 (PRE-SHAPED PLUS) 32", 34".

25/-

IN WHITE AND BLACK

Made under licence from Peter Pan Foundations Inc., New York by Corsets Silhouette Ltd., London, W.1

Prion Books Ltd. Imperial Works, Perren Street, London NW5 3ED
for information email humour@prion.co.uk • image courtesy of the advertising archives

Reduce
Exquisitely, Sanely and Safely
Nemolastik
Rubber Girdles and Brassieres

Exquisitely, because of the specially fine rubber, covered on both sides with very absorbent silk of peaches and cream shade. Protected Nemo garments dainty as silken lingerie.

* * *

Safely because no rubber touches the skin; and the figure is healthfully supported and controlled.

* * *

Sanely because the continuous auto-massage furnished by the elastic action of Nemolastik gradually eliminates excess fatty tissue and produces from the start a fashionable slenderness of appearance.

* * *

Nemolastik Girdles and Brassieres designed and made by the Master Makers of Nemo Corsets are the corset sensation of the fashion world. Guaranteed against tearing. Give long service and easily washed.

Cannot "Ride-Up"
Exclusive "Stayput" device on back of brassiere fastens securely to eyelets on girdle (see cut at left) and positively prevents brassieres from riding up over top of girdle.

Ask for them today at your dealers or fill in and forward attached coupon.

None Genuine Without This Mark:

Made of Genuine **Nemolastik** Letters Patent and Registration Pending.

BRASSIERE
$5 75

GIRDLE
$10 75

Nemo
THE HOUSE OF COMPLETE CORSETRY
120 EAST 16TH STREET
NEW YORK, N.Y.

Prion Books Ltd. Imperial Works, Perren Street, London NW5 3ED
for information email humour@prion.co.uk • image courtesy of the advertising archives

Ad Nauseam

Wake up
tomorrow as a

Model girl

Enjoy the fabulous feeling of fashion and freedom in this wonderful girdle. Flowing elastic panel controls hips and tummy and keeps you excitingly slim. "Model Girl" is for *you*, at only

45/-

White, trimmed with ice-blue embroidery.
Small, Medium, Large.

Styled by Perma-lift of New York.

Prion Books Ltd. Imperial Works, Perren Street, London NW5 3ED
for information email humour@prion.co.uk • image courtesy of the advertising archives

Ad
Nauseam

Prion Books Ltd. Imperial Works, Perren Street, London NW5 3ED
for information email humour@prion.co.uk • image courtesy of the advertising archives

Ad Nauseam

Shop for the Shade

in coloured *Nylon* lingerie
— it's a fashion MUST!

Slips and petticoats to match, to tone! Now in a rainbow-choice of colours from subtle to sensational, right in fashion, right in price— they're *nylon*. Team them with your autumn outfits—have *lots* of pretty nylon things. You really can't get by without them!

BRITISH NYLON SPINNERS LIMITED

Prion Books Ltd. Imperial Works, Perren Street, London NW5 3ED
for information email humour@prion.co.uk • image courtesy of the advertising archives

Ad
Nauseam

Prion Books Ltd. Imperial Works, Perren Street, London NW5 3ED
for information email humour@prion.co.uk • image courtesy of the advertising archives